Not Progressing...

My Issues are Leaking!

By: Christine Wilson

ACKNOWLEDGMENTS

I thank God for my mom because she has always told me to push through and do my best in everything I do. Thank you very much dad for supporting me in every way you could. My parents always told me to keep up the good work. To my sisters, Crystal W, Jennifer W, and Jennifer M. I just want to say thank you ladies for being a shoulder to lean and depend on and encouraging me.

To my nieces and godchildren, thank you for always believing and supporting me. To all my aunts, uncles, and cousins, I just want to say thank you for your words of encouragement. Tabernacle of Faith and Praise Worship Center:

I thank God for my Bishop Andrew Wells Sr. and First Lady Patricia Wells for teaching and training me to be the best me I can be. Pastor Andrew Wells Jr. and Lady Marva Wells, thank you for always praying and encouraging me to continue to go forth in all God have for me to do. To my prayer partners, sisters, brother, and friends, thank you for praying, encouraging, and supporting me to continue to move forward.

TABLE OF CONTENTS

CHAPTER ONE

Issues that Cause Struggles

I had many issues that caused me to have many struggles. My way of thinking was very unclear because I allowed my issues to overtake me; one is being under weight to overweight. This has caused me to have many struggles because at one point I was underweight with issues that I had to endure. I had some limitations I experienced that made me feel bad about being underweight growing up.

I had an incident that occurred that caused me to add more issues on me. I was 12 years old and my mom wanted me to do my house chores when I got home. However, I didn't do them right away. When I realized she was on her way home, I mopped the floor real fast and slipped on the tile floor. I got up hopping because I was in pain. My mom came home and asked why I was hopping and my sister told my mom the whole story. My mom started yelling at me. She was angry and said, "This is what happens when you don't listen to what you were told to do." I was still in pain, so my mom told me, "Soak your leg and go lay down."

I did that, but still was feeling the pain. I went back crying telling my mom it really hurt.

My mom was tired from working all day, but I kept coming back to my mom crying in so much pain. She took me to the hospital. Once we arrived, they took x-rays and noticed that I broke my hip. All because I didn't listen. This incident changed my life. They had to do emergency surgery because I broke my hip in two places. After surgery the doctor said, "The surgery went well." Now it was time for the healing process to begin.

I had to be in a wheelchair for ten weeks. At that point, I was limited to what I could do. I kept going back and forth to the refrigerator for food where I found comfort. That's when I started gaining weight. All I wanted to do was eat all day. I didn't exercise at all. I just found myself stuck in a wheelchair. It came to a point where it was time for me to start therapy. I couldn't wait until my therapy sessions were over, so I decided to cheat to finish up fast. I thought I was winning, but in reality, I was hurting myself which caused my left foot to become dysfunction even as of now.

However, I did start back walking after I completed therapy, but not like I use to walk before my incident because I didn't listen to my therapist. By then, I gained 75 pounds which caused another issue, this issue was weight gain. I gained too much weight while recovering from my incident. The weight started weighing me down. No matter how I tried to shake it or deal with it, I still face this every day of my life. The struggles and the pains are real. This caused me not to respect myself or like myself. I had no confidence, no motivation, and no endurance. At this point, I did not care about much. I didn't fully understand my circumstances, but one thing for sure it caused me to feel angry. I began to react to what I was going through.

My mom and dad always told me that I am a miracle child. I didn't feel like that because I couldn't get pass what I was going through or feeling. I experienced this daily. I felt very alone even though there were many people around me all the time. I felt sad, alone, and defeated. I was letting my situation get the best of me. My mom always told me, "God saw fit for you to live." As much as she told me that I felt a little better. It encouraged me throughout the years.

Now, moving forward to my adult hood and still dealing with my health issues of being overweight which cause me to have more issues. These issues included having high blood pressure, diabetes, and my asthma returned. I had to adapt to taking medicine. It put me in a place of frustration and fear. I thought I was too young to be on medicine, but I allowed food to overtake me. And when I should've started losing weight, I kept gaining more weight. It caused me to have low self-esteem, no motivation, no endurance which put me in a place to where I didn't care how I looked anymore. I wouldn't look in a mirror or take pictures. I wouldn't do the things that I needed to do for my body because I was mad, angry, and bitter with me. I didn't like who I had become. I still was bitter because of what I was going through.

Finally, I reached a turning point when I went back to the doctor. The doctor told me, "All your results are good, but one thing you need to do is lose weight and make better eating choices. This will cause your numbers to improve for your diabetes." I left the doctor and started working on my health right away. I wasn't going to allow my health to control me anymore. I was ready to take full control. I started to become true to myself and decided to exercise for me. I also made better eating choices. I begin to do a lifestyle change. I won't say that it's been easy, but every day I work harder than the day before. I would write affirmations and speak them into the atmosphere.

For instance, I will live and not die. I will declare the works of the Lord in the land of the living. This too shall pass. Theses affirmations helped me to stay encouraged and motivated. I begin to like me a little more. I was respecting me a little more. I understood that I can't allow my situation to control me from getting to my destiny. When I begin to grab hold of the real picture, I saw major changes within myself. I stop allowing my issues to control me. I begin to love me.

My issues have been leaking which has caused me to be behind in many areas of my life. We all have issues and struggles. Struggles comes to all of us in one way or another. It's not depending on the struggles, it's on how you handle the struggle.

My struggle is not going to be the same as yours, but you must turn your struggles over to God. He will be able to give you wisdom on how to handle it. I often struggle from day- to-day because I wanted to do things in my own strength. I know that if I allow God to take me through the process, I won't keep having to be tripped up with the same things I keep dealing with.

The struggles that I was dealing with had a major effect on me. One thing for sure was me being underweight to overweight. I became mean, but today I'm proud to say that I'm kind and humble. Don't allow your situations to dictate your future. You won't always be where you are.

Always remember in this life there will always be things that we have to go through. There will be many lessons we will learn. It's not to break us but to teach us, strengthen us, and build character. It will keep us teachable and humble. God knows us better than anybody. He still has His hands on you and I.

You are special! You are worth it! You are needed! I always want you to remember you are valuable! You are somebody! Keep shining pass your issues and struggles. God isn't finish with me yet and the best awaits you and I. We must let God heal all of our issues.

PRAYER

For Struggles

Thank you, God, for life. God, I thank you for keeping me during all I am dealing with right now.

Please keep me from my bad choices which cause me to have unnecessary struggles. Help me to keep my mind and eyes on you. I need you like never before in my life. I arrest everything that's trying to keep me tied down, bound, frustrated, and unmotivated in Jesus name.

I bind fear, worrying, and anything else that would try to take me from the place where God has me. I need you to hold me, keep me, and strengthen me in every area in Jesus name. Amen

REFLECTION

You may be going through something similar in your own life. What ways would you come out from being stuck?

PRAYER JOURNAL NOTES

CHAPTER TWO
People Pleaser

I became a people pleaser because of many undealt with issues. I allowed myself to sweep many things under the rug which allowed me to endure many unnecessary tests and trials. I allowed what people said to me to change what I was doing or where I was going because I just wanted to see everybody happy. This caused me not to progress on things I should have been doing.

I became comfortable and stagnated all at the same time. Which caused me to give lesser time for myself and more time for everything else that I thought was important. I begin to start sinking and losing myself. I begin to lose my "why" for life, purpose, and strength. My goals and dreams were left on the back burner. My job became number one. I would come to work early and leave late because I wanted to make everyone else happy.

I became angry, frustrated, exhausted, and very weary. This really bothered me a lot. It caused me to be vulnerable to my family and friends which I allowed them to persuade me to go places with them when I know I had many things I needed to do. I allowed every one's problem to become mines. Why did I allow this to take so much control over my whole life? I didn't want no one to think I was a selfish person. I had a lot of undealt with issues which caused me to have pity parties with myself.

I remember some years ago when God told me to break it off with my fiancé. God woke me up in the morning on New Year's Day in 2002. This day was one of the hardest days of my life. I had to prepare myself for what was ahead. I was scared and nervous because I really loved my ex-fiancé. I thought this was who God had for me for the rest of my life. I thought, there were much soul ties that was created which made it more difficult for what I was about to do.

I begin to rehearse and rehearse in my mind because I didn't want to cause no damage from me. I begin to talk to myself on how I was going to tell him. I was crying and in great anxiety of releasing this news to him. I didn't want him to think it was because I didn't love him or that I wanted to be with someone else. I wanted him to know that I fear God and this was a God thing.

One thing I had to realize in this life is when God tells you to do something you have to be obedient. I felt like I was losing because what God told me to do left me in a place of loneliness and uncertainty. It was because of what I saw with my eyes. At first, when it happened my ex-fiancé was calling me all the time asking me if I was sure that is what I heard from God. He would bring me flowers and stop by my house often as if I really didn't hear from God.

After a while everything started changing, the calls, flowers, and showing up to my house all stopped. I heard he was now dating someone else. I said to myself, "He got over me quick." I was a little in my feelings. Then I heard he was getting married. I said, "God this seems like I didn't hear you correctly because it appeared to me that he was winning, and I was losing. "Eventually, after his wedding he was expecting a baby. I begin to have so many mix emotions because I love children. I kept questioning God believing that I didn't hear Him correctly.

This caused me to draw back from God when I should have been drawing myself closer to God. I wasn't aware at the time that I was angry with God. All I wanted to do is to be love and live happily ever after.

One thing I realize is we never know why God tells us to do certain things. I learned that it was to save me from things unknown at that time.

For 18 years, I've decided to live a celibate life. Not saying, I don't get tempted or alone at times. I decided to truly wait on God. I realize that while I've been single, I've been able to accomplish somethings that I should've accomplished early on. I've learned that I can't allow people to steal my time no more. I had to take full control and now I'm moving forward in my life. I had to learn how to stop letting people use and abuse me. It's okay for me to say "No". Many people through the years took my kindness for weakness.

PRAYER

For People Pleasers

Lord, I thank you for breaking the cycle that had control over me. I thank you for keeping me and my mind when I was angry, confuse, frustrated, overwhelmed, and not producing.

God, I thank you for giving me the strength that I need to continue to grow. When I was not motivated, you gave me what I needed. When I was lost, you, gave me direction. I thank you for continually keeping me to keep my eyes stayed on you.

Lord, I ask you to continue to allow me to stay humble before you in every area of my life. Lord, I thank you for releasing me from being a people pleaser. In Jesus name.

REFLECTION

You may be going through something similar in your own life. What strategies will you use when you find yourself people pleasing?

PRAYER JOURNAL NOTES

CHAPTER THREE
Pain

The pain has allowed me to become stuck and not progressing. Day in and day out the same pain and the same cycle every day. I had allowed someone to make me feel like I was not good enough or worthy. This made me feel low and unappreciated. It hurt me to the core. I felt as if my life was out of control because of the way people made me feel. I allowed the devil to have a field day with my mind. I begin to be uninterested in the things that really matter to me because of the hurt which I allowed it to harden my heart. I allowed the devil to use me by allowing me to stop doing what I love to do. I continued to be mad, angry, confuse, frustrated, bitter, shattered and even felt worthless. I asked, "God why is it that this has happened to me?" I was helping people, praying for people, being faithful, coming to Bible study, and doing all I was supposed to do in reference to what was expected of me.

I felt like I was not good enough and overlooked at times. I was there when people needed me to get something done or if someone needed me individually. I begin to shy away from things I know I should be doing. I started doing bear minimum. My heart was heavy. My heart was full. My heart was not ready to be healed. I thirst so long hurting. Not understanding or knowing who I had become because of this deep hurt I had been carrying. I was trying to accept what has happened to me and move on. I tried to break free, but I kept getting stuck. I was wrapped up in my issues.

Many times, I relied on people to complete me or even to take the pain away. I tried to push myself to pray, but I couldn't with all of the roller coaster of emotions. I allowed someone to get in my head. I was my own distraction. I couldn't read my devotions, scriptures, pray or sleep. I didn't even really have an appetite. I couldn't even talk without crying because of the pain. I have many brothers and sisters in the gospel, but I felt like no one was able to catch me in the spirit or reach out to me. I just long for someone to say, "Girl, I see you hurting let me pray with you" or even call to encourage me. The pressure of life was trying to make me quit by making me think it was not worth it. One thing I had to do is repent and forgive me then forgive the ones who hurt me.

I had to keep my focus on God, have faith, and know that God will see me through. Let God make a way through the issues, the tests, and trials. When your mind is all over the place and you feel defeated, be steadfast and trust God with all your heart. What is in your heart will come out good or bad. I learned through all of this to continue to stay in prayer and fasting to keep myself in full fellowship with God and not so much focus on people. We must remember to take authority, and declare and decree total wholeness over everything that is trying to take control. I must continue to hold on to God's hand. I have to trust Him and not my own understanding. I must let go and let God!

PRAYER

For Pain

Lord, I am totally broken right now. I am a mess right now in my life Lord. Lord I need you. I come to you the only way I know how. Lord I come to you concerning the hurt I feel from the pain. Am sick and tired of the way I've been feeling. Lord I need you to break every cycle of the pain that has attach itself to me in Jesus name.

I come against every high thing that's trying to control my mind, and my life. Lord I ask you to heal me, set me free from the pain and everything else that comes with it that I have held on to. The pain that keeps me sad, angry, frustrated, weary, and bitter, Lord break the power in Jesus name. Lord I need you to continue to keep my mind, heart, and every being of me stayed on you. I need you right now Lord. I am tired of allowing myself to have these adult tantrums. Lord I have allowed someone to cause pain to me, and I allowed the pain to control me long enough.

Lord, I need you to forgive me for what I have allowed. Lord I cry out to you in Jesus name to revive me. Lord please keep me, teach me to walk and live in wholeness in Jesus name.

I need you to totally heal me from the hurt, the pain that I allowed to cause a manifestation in my heart. Lord please don't allow me to continue to live like this no more. Please restore me and allow me to be set free. In Jesus name! Amen

REFLECTION

You may be going through something similar in your own life. How will you overcome the pain?

PRAYER JOURNAL NOTES

CHAPTER FOUR

How Did I Get Here!?

I'm single at the moment because I choose not to compromise what I believe. I could have been married, but because I choose to follow the voice of God. I had to realize that I have to follow the instructions of God and not people. God is real and is a very jealous God. God desires for us to live a total surrender life.

God will heal, deliver, set free, and restore all things, but I had to first acknowledge my problem. My problem that I had was low self-esteem which caused me to do and react to things in a negative way. I had to respect, love, and value myself. I didn't even realize I had gotten to this point in my life. Doing things out of my character and accepting things that I should not have.

I allowed myself to get very bitter and hold resentment because of my issues at the time. I had to realize that I couldn't remain in the same place I was in. I had to work on me which included doing more prayer, fasting, reading, and studying God's word. I had to repeat this and turn from my ways. It wasn't easy at all. I failed many times, but I kept pushing and pressing.

When I begin to really seek God, it allowed me to not just be talking about what I'm doing, but living it to the fullest. I had to take my eyes off what I saw and heard. Many people were single, but living and saying things contrary to God's word. I had to pray harder because sometimes the enemy will try to use people to get you off track. Many times, I've done things because of what I've seen and not by following God's instructions.

I allowed many people to hold me back because of my insecurities and fears of the unknown. I had to continue to seek God in season and out of season. I had to trust and believe everything God was doing inside of me. I had to take my eyes totally off everyone and solely rely on Jesus. He was the only one who could get me out of what I allowed myself to get in.

PRAYER

For Following God's Instructions

I thank you God for helping me to keep my eyes on you. Thank you for helping me to study and show myself approve. Continue to lead and guide me in the way I should go. I need you to continue to have your way in my life.

God, help me to live each day and follow your instructions. I have failed many times, but I kept persevering myself through. I need you to continue to cover and protect me. In Jesus Name. Amen!

REFLECTION

You may be going through something similar in your own life. How will you follow God's instructions?

PRAYER JOURNAL NOTES

CHAPTER FIVE
Moving Forward

There are some things that I had to do to move forward in life. I couldn't stay stagnate in the things that use to trip me up. I couldn't continue to let the same things continue to have control over me. I had to first let go of fear and release it to God and allow God to heal me from fear.

Secondly, I had to let go of people pleasing because it was wearing me down. I had to get free from the heavy weight that I was carrying. I had to accept where I was and how I got here, so I could continue to move forward in life.

Thirdly, I had to build motivation because I had none to create to get me out from my stuck place. I had to confront, deal with it, and set goals to continue to move forward from being stuck. These are the steps that I took to break free from what was holding me back from moving forward.

Confront

I had to come face to face with what I was dealing with. I had to embrace the issues and allow myself time to work myself through these things I had to confront. It took time for me to address the issues. I didn't want to rush through them. I had to face head on what was keeping me from achieving. I had to face reality that it is what it is. I had to come in grips with what I had to confront.

Deal With It

I had to come to the reality what I was up against. I had to lay everything out to continue to work through it. I had to understand that what I don't deal with, it will keep me stuck, frustrated, mad, angry, bitter and it goes on and on. I had to acknowledge and attack that thing head on that's how I was able to deal with what's been keeping me from moving forward.

Setting Goals

I had to learn how to set healthy and realistic goals. I started by setting daily goals, weekly goals, monthly goals, quarterly goals, and yearly goals. Following through and staying true with my goals. I had to set deadlines for each goal to be completed. Set goals that are realistic, achievable, and reachable. I had to learn that goals are important in life.

Goals also allow you to organize your time. Goals allow you to measure your process. Goals make you accountable and help you to complete the task. Goals give you motivation. Goals allow you to get active and keep you focus. Goals allow you to start achieving.

PRAYER

For Moving Forward

God, I thank you for having your way in my life. Lord I thank you for breaking off everything that had me entangled. Lord, I thank you that it's you that have been giving me the strategies to move forward. Thank you that you continue to give me strength to go through day to day.

Thank you, Lord, for allowing me to be awaken from being stuck and moving forward. God, I thank you that you keep allowing me to have wisdom and understanding to keep moving forward. Lord, I thank you that I'm focus and attentive to continue to progress. In Jesus' name. Amen.

REFLECTION

You may be going through something similar in your own life. How will you move forward?

PRAYER JOURNAL NOTES

CHAPTER SIX
Holding On to God's Promises

I am holding on to the promises God has told me. Not saying that this journey has been easy. When you see what's before you and it doesn't appear to be lining up, I had to continue to have faith and not doubt what God promised. This is not the time for me to give up.

God had to remind me that He will make room for me. The promise said, "The struggles are over." In the natural, I saw nothing but struggles. God told me, "I had to change my vision because what I was doing was my vision and not God's vision." Then I begin to start seeing God's promises.

Here's a few declarations that has helped me to continue to push, persevere, and stay encourage:

DECLARATIONS

'I will Live and NOT Die and be in Good Health!'

'Don't be Entangled from the Yoke of Bondage!'

'I am FREE!'

'It isn't over Yet!'

'What God has in store is going to be BIGGER than my Past!'

'I will NEVER be broke again!'

'My heart's desires WILL come to pass!'

The same thing God has told me, I know many of you are right here, right now in your life. Keep the faith and don't waver in waiting. Know that what you are carrying is way more than what you have receive or settled for. You will excel and achieve in everything God has for you to do.

PRAYER

For God's Promises

Thank you, Lord, for allowing your promises that you have promise to give me hope and assurance to come alive in my spirit. I thank you for allowing your will to be done in my life. Thank you, God, that it's you that allow me to be able to have faith and believe that you going to do all you have promised. Please keep my mind and heart stayed on You.

Thank you for allowing me wisdom to trust your word for my life. Lord, I thank you that you will give me my heart desires. Thank you for allowing me to hold on to your word. When I can't chase you, I can still trust you. Thank you for making room for me. Thank you that the struggles are over. Even when they arise it don't have control over me no more. I thank you that you have giving us power to call things into existence in so let it be. I call good health in Jesus name. I will no longer be entangled to bondage.

I am free from all that keeps me from my promises. God, I thank you for what I'm carrying is far more than what I received. Thank you, God, for moving by your spirit in my life. Amen.

REFLECTION

What has God promised you?

PRAYER JOURNAL NOTES

"YOU ARE"

Inspirations

You are worth it!

You are worthy!

You are nice.

You are sweet.

You are special.

You are a great value.

You are an achiever.

You are beautiful inside and out.

You are handpicked.

You are unique.

You are needed.

You are important.

You are loved.

You are appreciated.

You are kind.

No one to compare to who you are.

There's no guess why you rock!

PRAYER JOURNAL NOTES

"I AM"

Inspirations

I Am somebody.

I Am a conqueror.

I Am grateful.

I Am determined.

I Am intelligent.

I Am blessed.

I Am capable.

I Am unique.

I Am creative.

I Am a survivor of self.

I Am an overcomer.

PRAYER JOURNAL NOTES

KEEP PUSHING & DON'T STOP

Inspirations

Keep pushing.

Don't stop pushing.

Don't stop praying.

Don't stop working on you.

Don't stop moving.

Don't stop producing.

Don't stop exceling.

Don't stop achieving.

Don't stop fighting.

Don't quit.

Keep Progressing in all you do!

PRAYER JOURNAL NOTES

38

MOVING

Inspirations

Motivating ourselves to continue

Overcoming any obstacles that tries to get us from maintaining

Value and knowing our worth to continue to overcome and dominating

Issues that tries to keep us from not moving push through and don't let them stop you

Navigating us to achieve

Greatness to keep us moving.

Moving keeps us motivated to continue to overcome different things that tries to keep us from moving and not understanding our value. There are times when we have unnecessary issues, but we must keep navigating ourselves through. We must continue to keep moving and stay focus.

PRAYER JOURNAL NOTES

WHEN YOU ARE STUCK

Inspirations

"When you are Stuck" Inspirations

Support yourself

Triumph over your issues

Understand the process

Change your mind from a defeat mentality

Knowledge is important to keep you from being stuck

We must continue to support ourselves. Stay open and free from whatever had us trapped in the past. Be teachable and be ready to triumph over your issues. Also, understand the process and be willing to change, so you will not stay stuck or become stuck again. The knowledge that you have gained will allow you to know the importance of keeping it moving.

PRAYER JOURNAL NOTES

PROGRESSING

Inspirations

Pushing to continue to progress

Responsible to take ownership to keep progressing

Optimistic to achieve progressing

Growth to continue to grow through the progress

Result from what was learned from progressing.

Embracing and emerging through

PRAYER JOURNAL NOTES

SUPPORT

INSPIRATIONS

'Succeed'

'Initiating Staying True to Progress'

'Necessary to Continue to Progress'

'Gain Knowledge from What I Have Learned from Progressing'

Everyone needs support. When you have the support, you will succeed as well as initiating true progress to where you are. It is necessary for support because it keeps you encourage and inspired.

You also gain knowledge from what was learned through the progress.

PRAYER

Lord, I thank you for allowing me to recognize my issues that caused me to remain stuck in my life. Thank you for allowing me to see what was causing me not to progress. Lord, I thank you for being a keeper. Thank you, Lord, for all you are doing right now. You alone are worthy of all my praise. I give you all the praise Lord. You are worthy Lord. You keep my mind stayed on you. I need you, every second, every minute, every hour, and every day. I thank you for all I've been through.

Please, God continue to keep and hold me in every way. You provide for me in many ways. You continue to make a way for me and give me provision and wisdom. You are worthy Lord. Thank you, Lord, for all you are doing. You are an amazing God. I love you. I can't make it without you. After all I have been through, and yet going through you keep on keeping me. There is none like you God. Please continue to help me stay focus on myself so I can continue to grow in you. Please keep me from the snares that easily tries to keep me entangled and not producing.

Please keep my eyes open. Please keep my ears de-clogged. Please keep my body healed and my body restored. Please keep my family and all around me covered in Jesus name. God please give me strength. Thank you, Lord, for all you are doing in me right now. You are worthy Lord. Lord, please continue to help me release people from keeping control over me. Please help me to move pass rejection that has control my life long enough. God, I ask you to continue to help me release fear, past hurts, and everything that controlled my life long enough. Please God continue to give me endurance to push and complete things you have for me to complete in this season in my life.

Please, God continue to give me motivation to continue to move, excel, and achieve in all you have for me to do. Lord, we thank you lord and we give you all the praise and honor for moving by your spirit. In your strong name I pray. So, let it be. Amen

From the Heart of the Author

My issues were leaking which caused me no progression in my life. Many of us are here right now in our life and some of us just past this point. We have experienced what I have shared. I encourage you to acknowledge your issue, confront your issue, and deal with your issue. Don't allow your issue to cause you to be stuck, not producing, and flat out of control. Take control of your life and continue to persevere. What helped me out tremendously was prayer and saying daily affirmations. I want you to stay strong and let God heal and restore all your issues. Release that hurt, pain, struggle, or issue you were holding on to, so they don't keep coming up. Let go and let God. Walk in your healing now.

Nothing but the best awaits YOU!!!

Meet the Author

'Christine Wilson'

Christine Wilson is the CEO/Founder of **Believe CW Life Coach,** she is a Certified Life Coach. She is an Ordained Minister and the Author of ***Through the Struggles***, How God change me. Christine is a woman with many talents and creative. She loves to see people excel to their full potential. With many tests and trials that she has experienced, Christine encourages people to excel and achieve in all they do.

This book is to encourage you, strengthen you, give hope to you, and to allow you to know that you can push through; even in the midst of issues, self, trials, stumbling blocks, obstacles, fear, past hurts, people pleaser, rejection, no endurance, no motivation, and anything that comes your way. Stay encourage and keep it moving. You will excel and achieve if you believe. You are worth it! You are needed! Continue to move forward! You are a winner! You are an achiever!

Connect with Christine on Facebook at Christine Nicole Wilson or follow Christine on her FB Business Page. Email: BelieveCWLifeCoach@gmail.com

9 7 9 8 5 8 8 5 7 2 3 6 1